You Are Loved!
Color By Number Coloring Book For Adults and Teens
Large Print Flowers, Hearts
And Short Inspirational Quotes about Love

BY COLOR QUESTOPIA

Copyright © 2021

All rights reserved. No part of this publication may be reproduced, distributed, or transmitted in any form or by any means, including photocopying, recording, or other electronic or mechanical methods, without the prior written permission of the publisher

Color By Number Tips

1. **Relax and have fun**
   Let your cares slip away as you color the images. Take your time. Coloring is a meditative activity and there's no wrong way to do it. Feel free to color as you listen to music, watch TV, lounge in bed- do whatever relaxes you most! You can also color while you're out and about- on the train or at a cafe- take the book with you anywhere you go. Coloring is therapeutic and is great for stress relief and relaxation!

2. **Colors corresponding to each number are shown on the back cover of the book - THIS BOOK HAS OUR NEW COLORING SYSTEM WHERE EVERY COLOR IN EVERY BOOK IS SHOWN ON THE BACK OF THE BOOK**
   Each number corresponds to a color shown on the back of the book. Because this is our new system, there may be colors and numbers on the back that aren't in this book- that's totally okay. Just follow the numbers on the images in this book, and match those numbers to colors. You can match the color as closely as you like- but feel free to change the color or the shade if you don't have the exact color match- that's totally fine. Although this is a color by number book, it's completely okay to get creative and color the images with whichever colors you like and have. The numbers are there to be a guide and to allow you to color without having to focus your energy on choosing colors.

3. **Choose your coloring tools**
   Everyone has their favorite coloring markers, crayons, pencils, pens- even paints! Feel free to color with any tool that you like! If you choose markers or paints, we recommend putting a blank sheet of paper or cardboard behind each image, so that your colors don't run onto the next image.

5. Red

8. Light Yellow

9. Yellow

11. Bright Orange

14. Orange

18. Medium Brown

21. Neon Green

22. Light Green

24. Green

26. Dark Green

28. Light Pink

29. Medium Pink

30. Pink

33. Medium Purple

35. Light Violet

39. Baby Blue

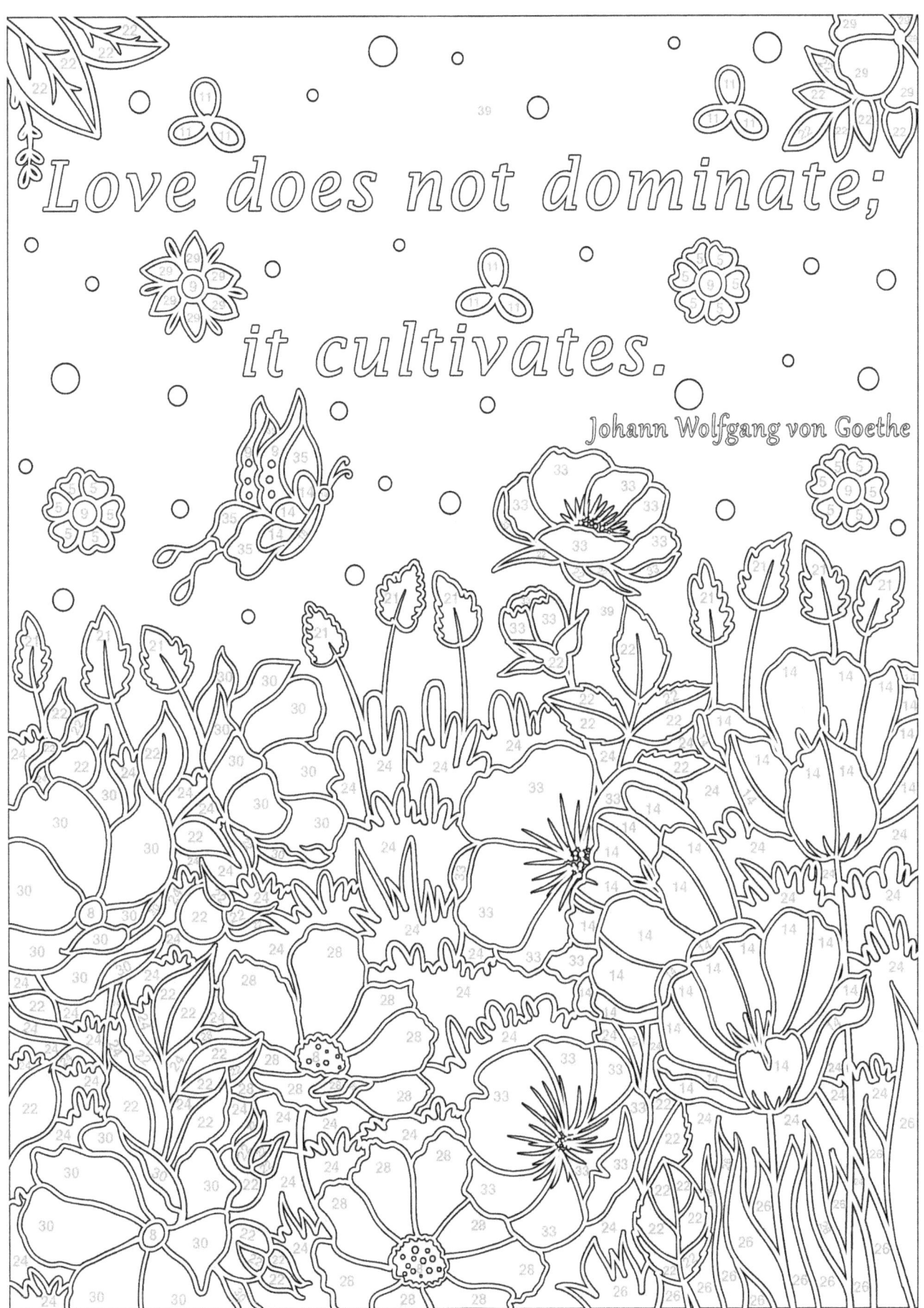

5. Red

7. Lemon Yellow

9. Yellow

21. Neon Green

22. Light Green

24. Green

25. Army Green

26. Dark Green

28. Light Pink

34. Purple

35. Light Violet

43. Blue

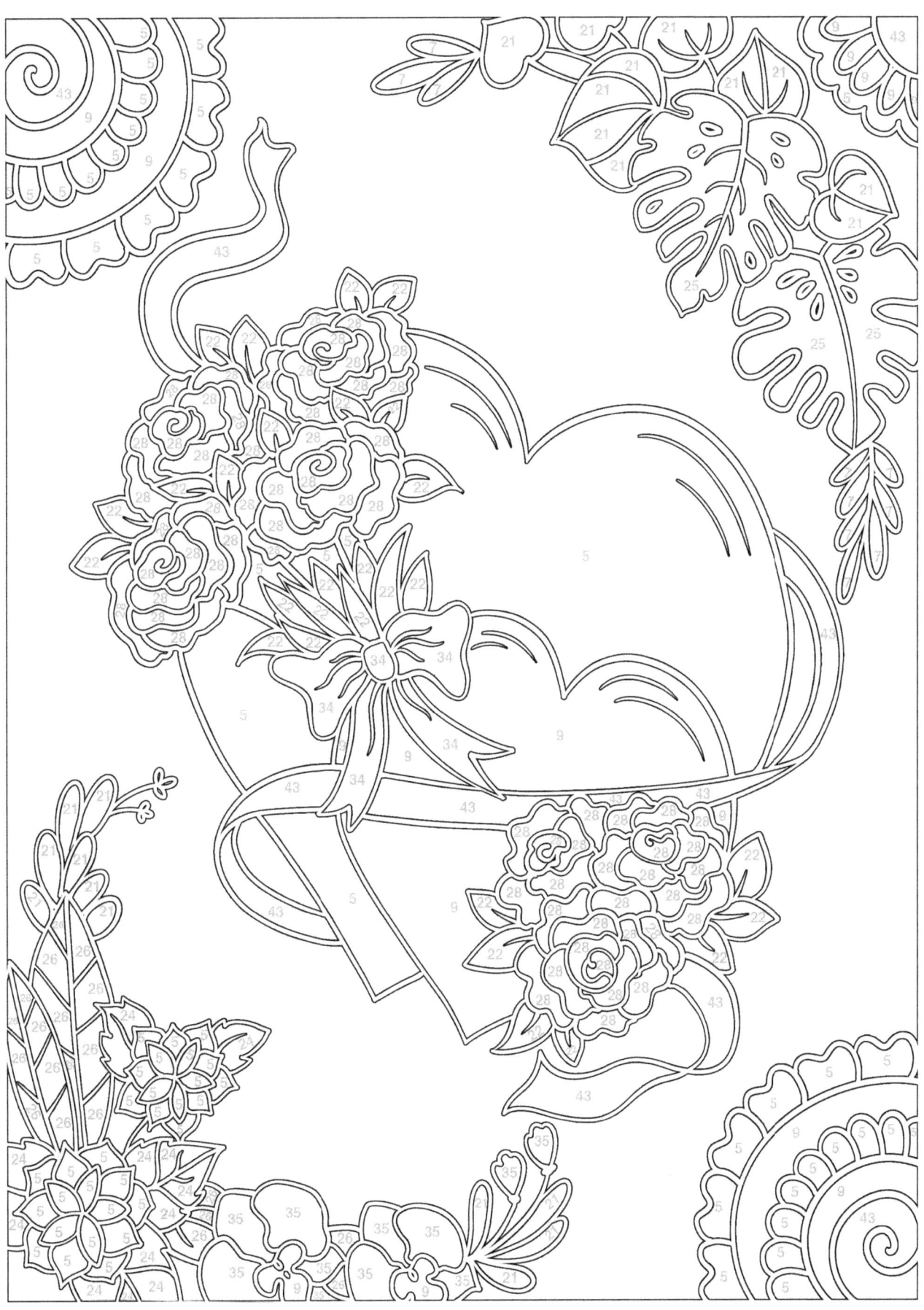

2. Golden

5. Red

9. Yellow

23. Medium Green

27. Peach

28. Light Pink

35. Light Violet

42. Medium Blue

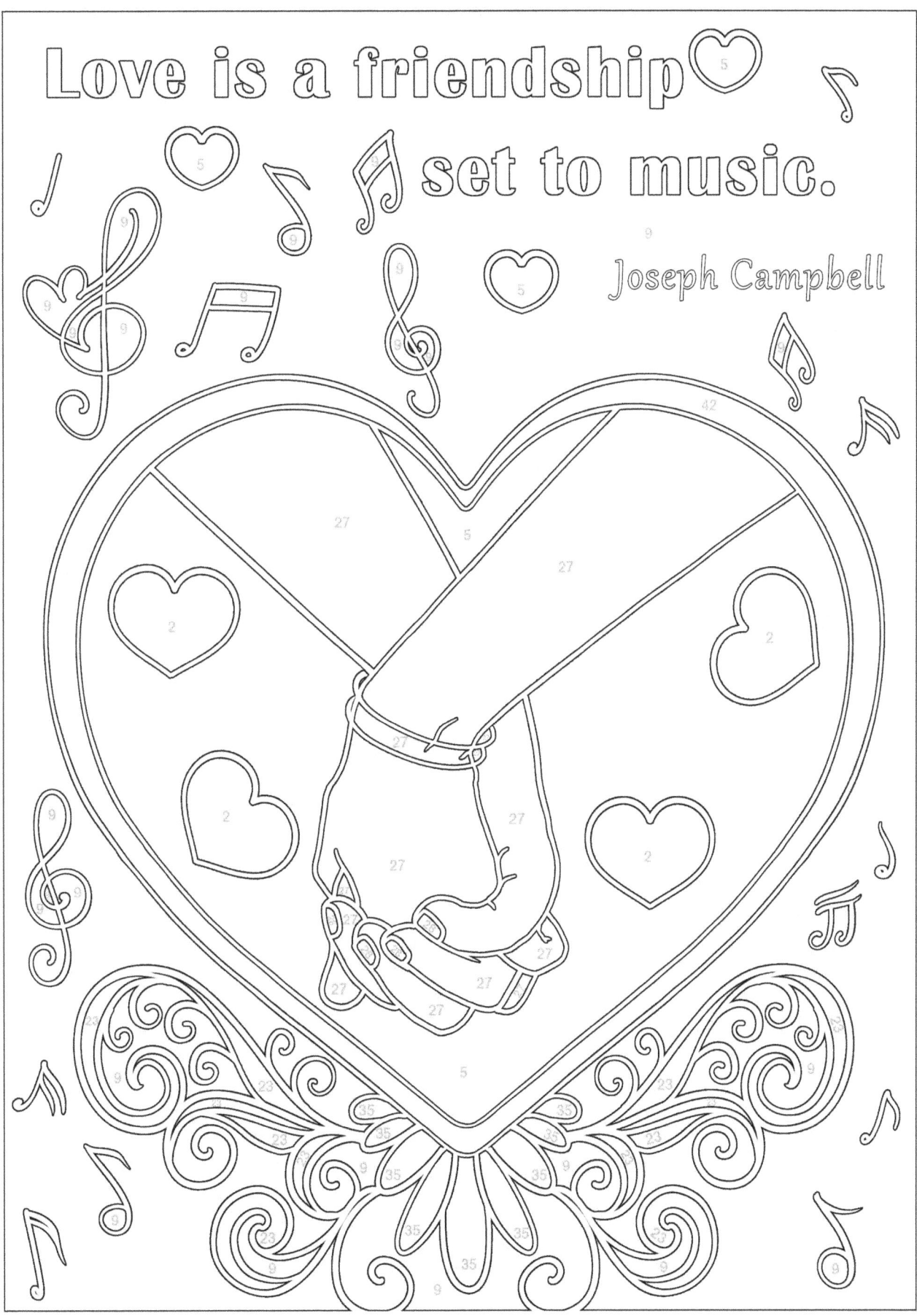

5. Red

9. Yellow

14. Orange

23. Medium Green

24. Green

25. Army Green

29. Medium Pink

30. Pink

34. Purple

37. Violet

3. Light Red

5. Red

9. Yellow

11. Bright Orange

12. Light Orange

14. Orange

22. Light Green

29. Medium Pink

35. Light Violet

45. Navy Blue

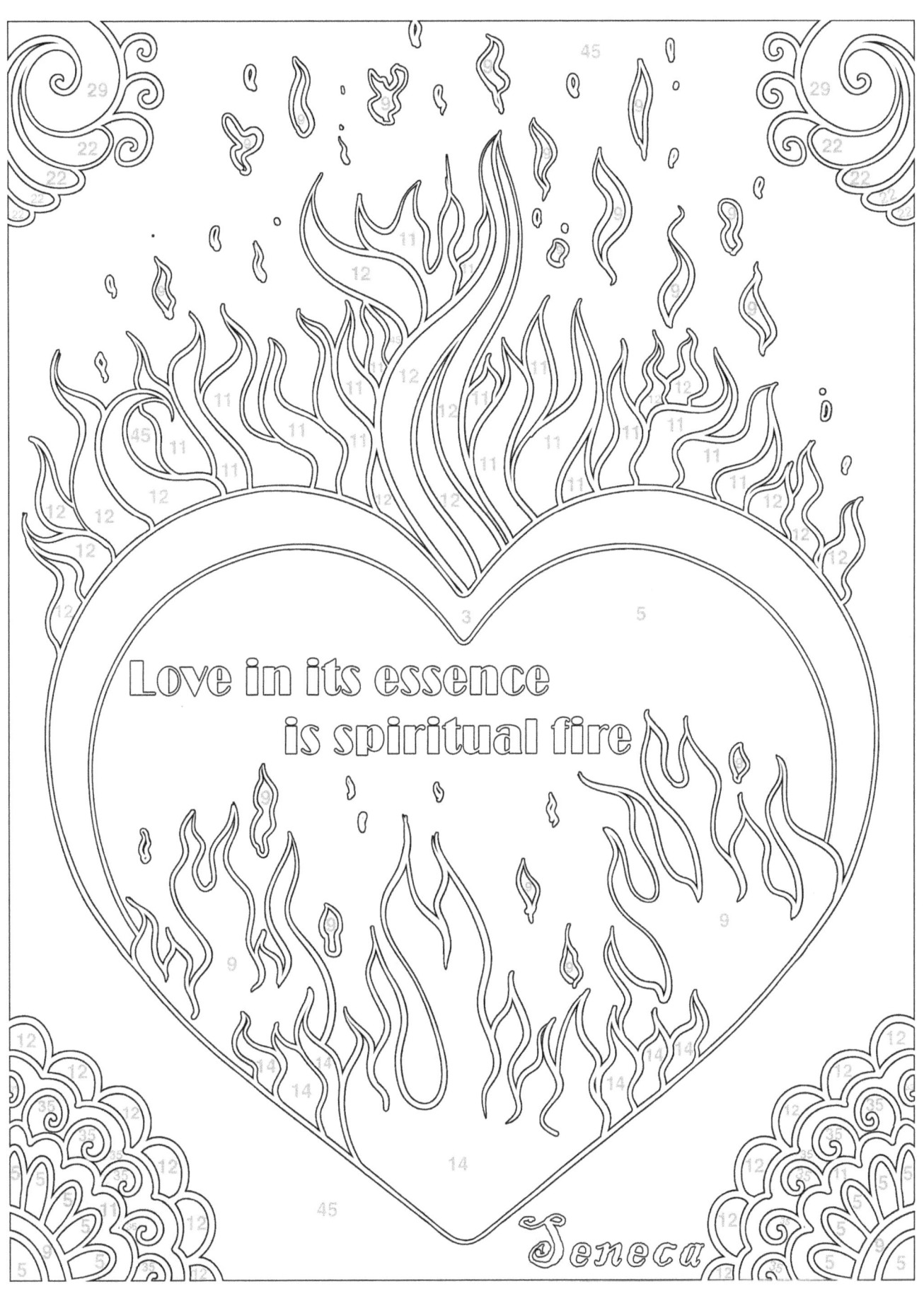

5. Red

9. Yellow

11. Bright Orange

12. Light Orange

24. Green

28. Light Pink

30. Pink

33. Medium Purple

34. Purple

37. Violet

42. Medium Blue

4. Medium Red

5. Red

6. Dark Red

9. Yellow

11. Bright Orange

17. Light Brown

18. Medium Brown

19. Brown

20. Dark Brown

22. Light Green

24. Green

26. Dark Green

28. Light Pink

30. Pink

39. Baby Blue

40. Sky Blue

41. Light Blue

47. Light Gray

48. Medium Gray

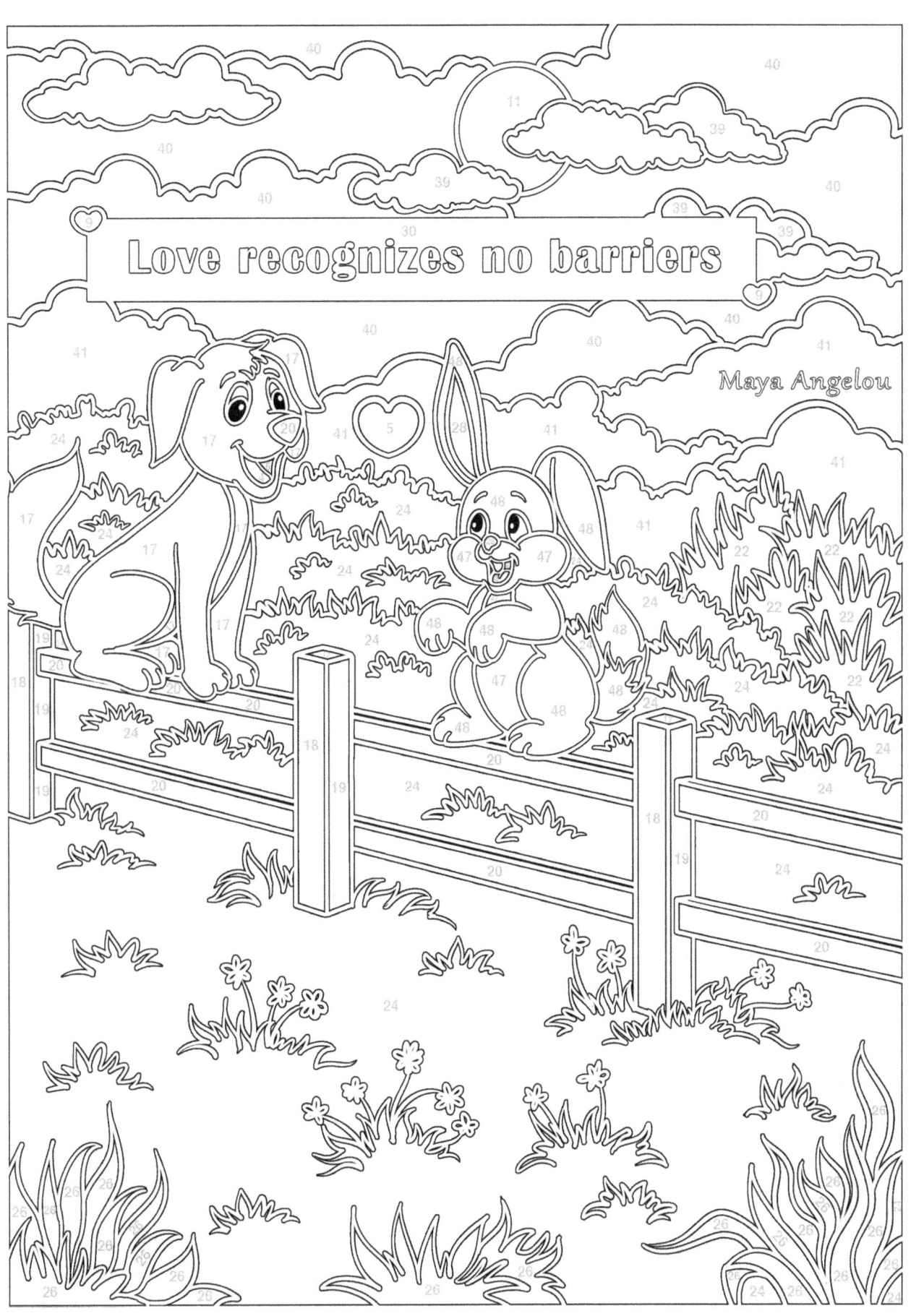

5. Red

9. Yellow

11. Bright Orange

14. Orange

22. Light Green

24. Green

28. Light Pink

31. Hot Pink

33. Medium Purple

34. Purple

35. Light Violet

37. Violet

38. Dark Violet

41. Light Blue

5. Red

9. Yellow

12. Light Orange

14. Orange

17. Light Brown

18. Medium Brown

19. Brown

21. Neon Green

22. Light Green

23. Medium Green

24. Green

26. Dark Green

30. Pink

37. Violet

40. Sky Blue

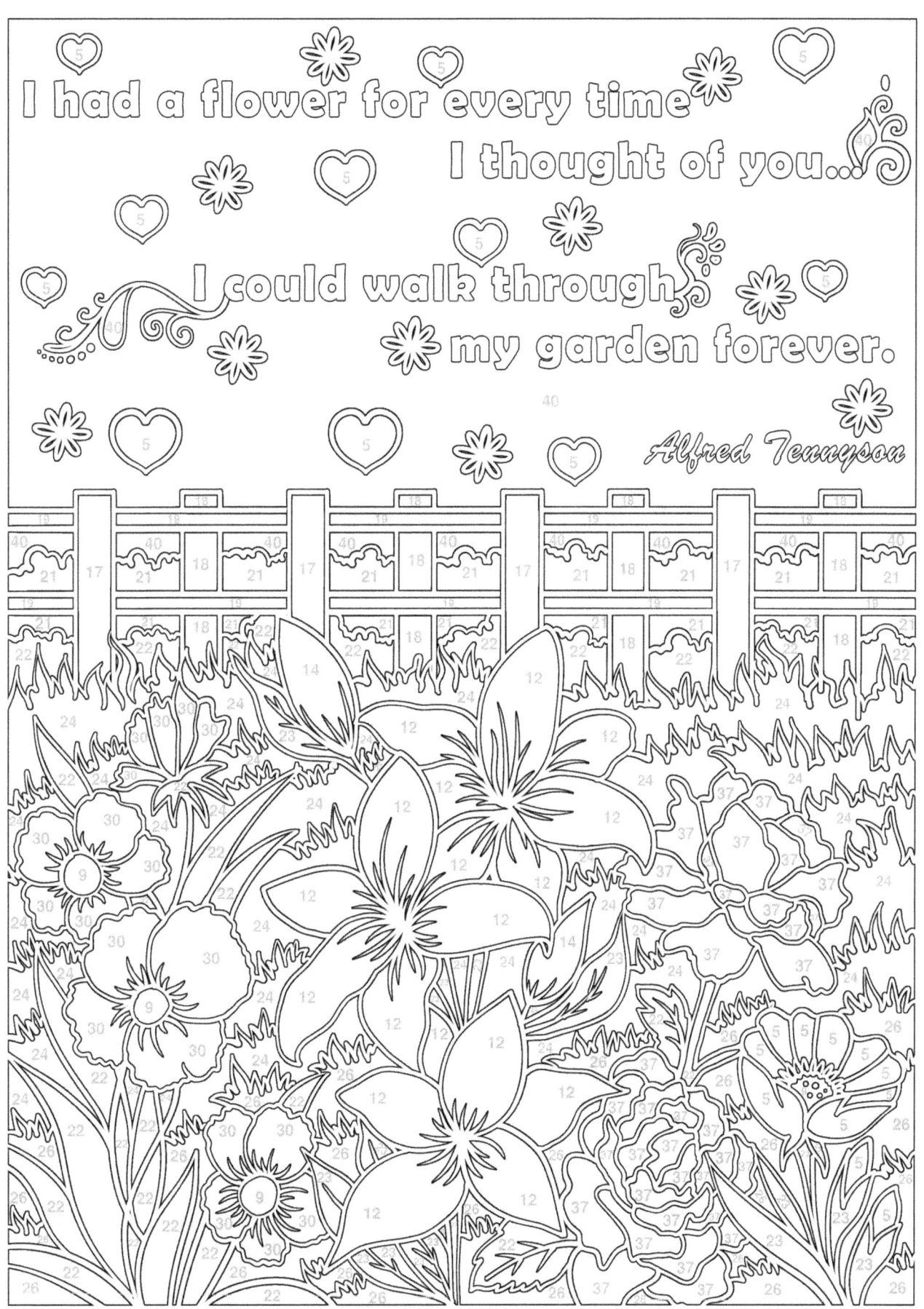

5. Red

9. Yellow

11. Bright Orange

12. Light Orange

14. Orange

21. Neon Green

24. Green

28. Light Pink

29. Medium Pink

35. Light Violet

2. Golden

5. Red

9. Yellow

18. Medium Brown

24. Green

31. Hot Pink

34. Purple

35. Light Violet

39. Baby Blue

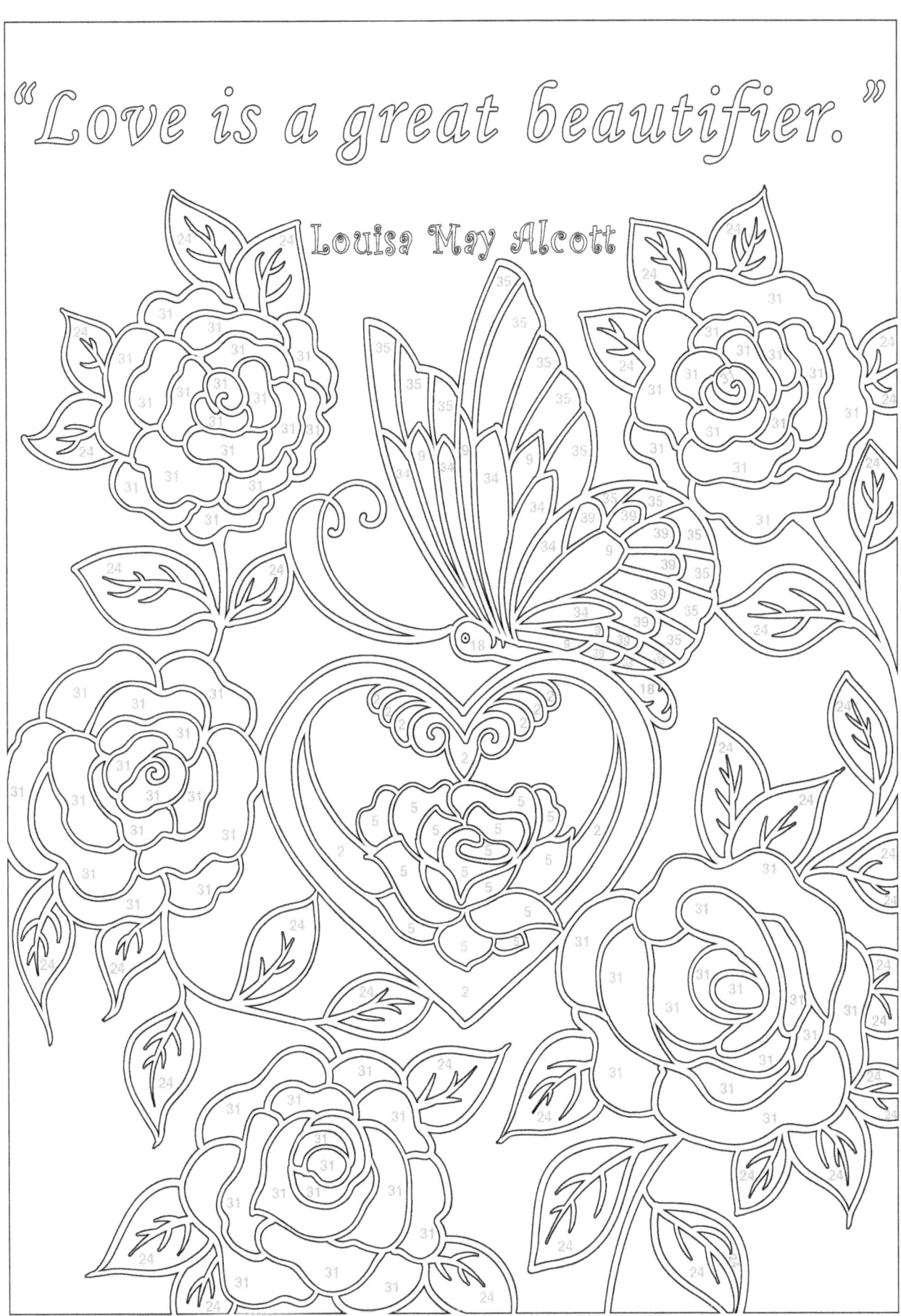

3. Light Red
5. Red
8. Light Yellow
9. Yellow
10. Dark Yellow
11. Bright Orange
13. Medium Orange
14. Orange
16. Chocolate
19. Brown
24. Green
26. Dark Green
28. Light Pink
30. Pink
33. Medium Purple

39. Baby Blue
43. Blue

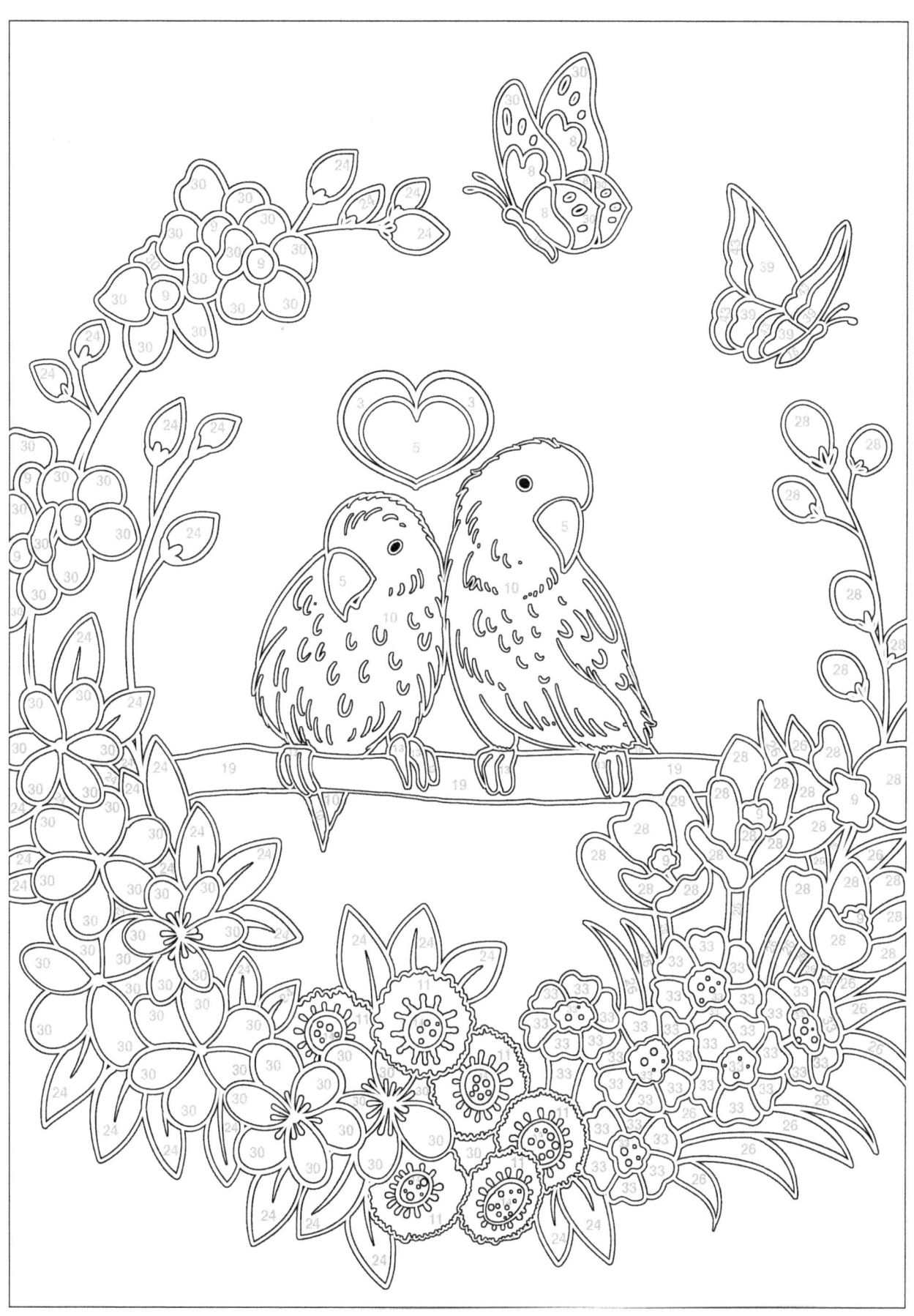

1. Black

5. Red

9. Yellow

13. Medium Orange

20. Dark Brown

22. Light Green

24. Green

27. Peach

28. Light Pink

34. Purple

37. Violet

39. Baby Blue

40. Sky Blue

43. Blue

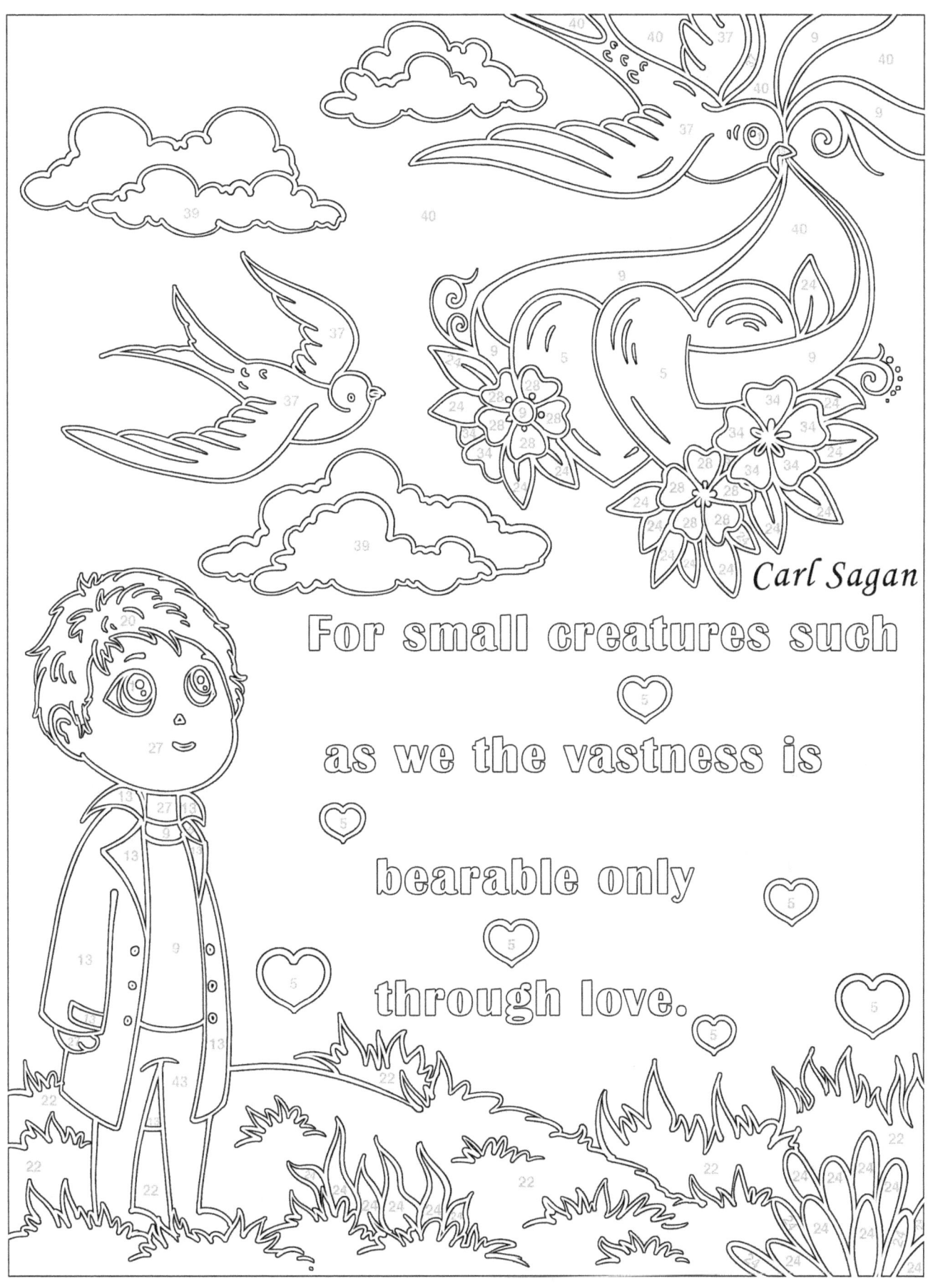

3. Light Red

5. Red

6. Dark Red

9. Yellow

14. Orange

23. Medium Green

24. Green

25. Army Green

28. Light Pink

30. Pink

37. Violet

5. Red

9. Yellow

12. Light Orange

14. Orange

16. Chocolate

22. Light Green

24. Green

28. Light Pink

30. Pink

33. Medium Purple

34. Purple

37. Violet

43. Blue

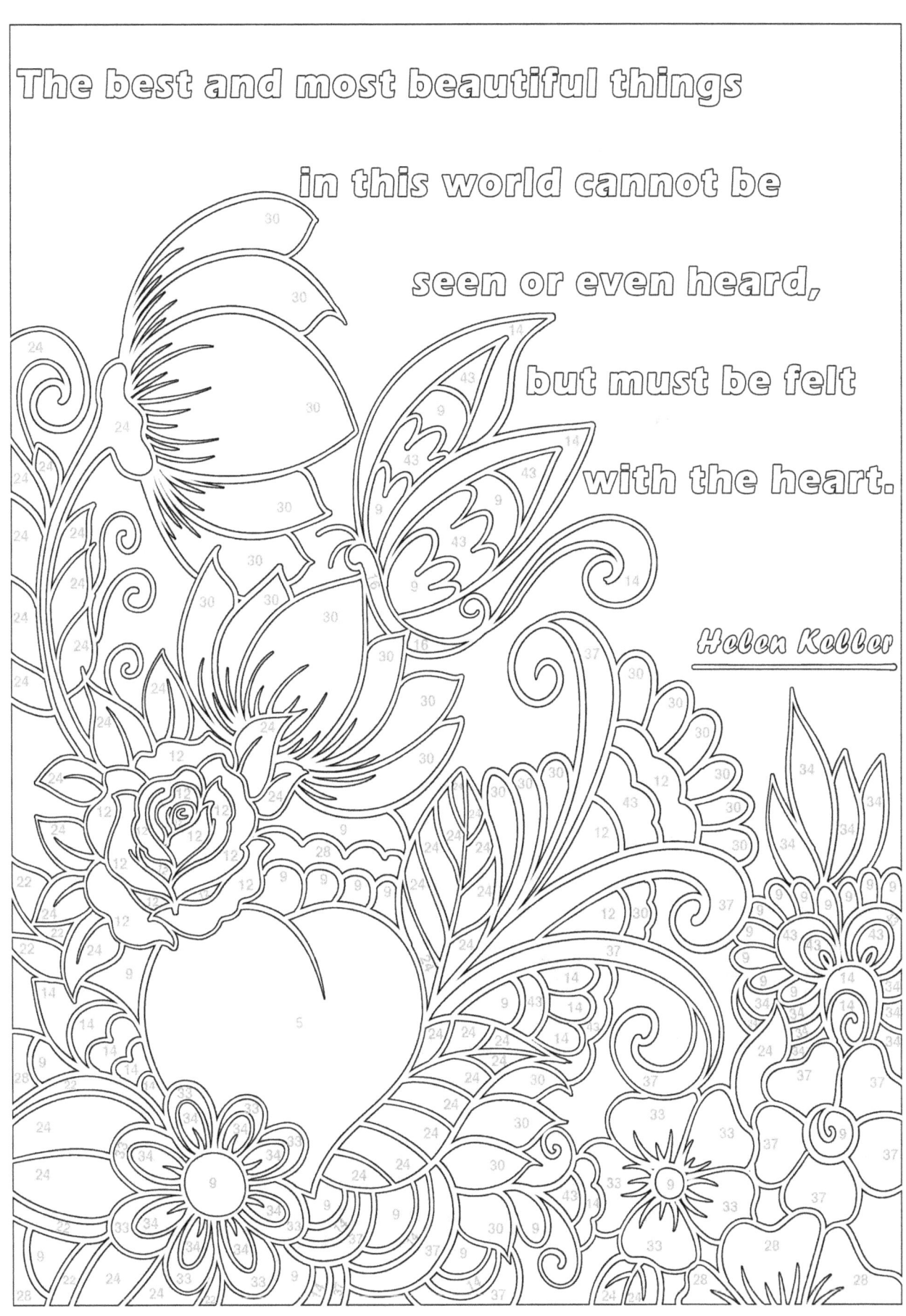

5. Red

7. Lemon Yellow

9. Yellow

14. Orange

18. Medium Brown

23. Medium Green

24. Green

28. Light Pink

30. Pink

34. Purple

35. Light Violet

43. Blue

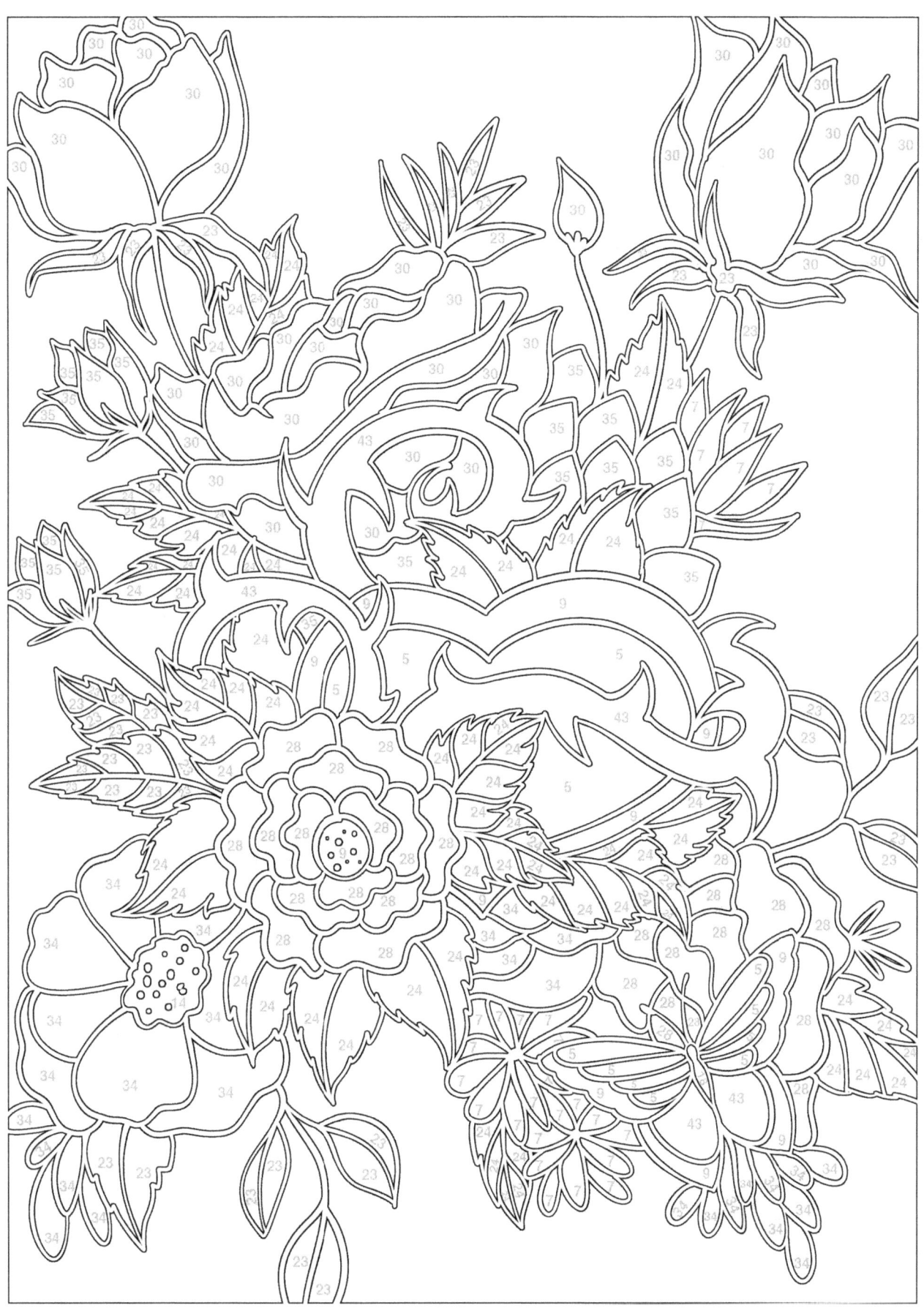

5. Red

6. Dark Red

7. Lemon Yellow

9. Yellow

11. Bright Orange

24. Green

28. Light Pink

30. Pink

31. Hot Pink

35. Light Violet

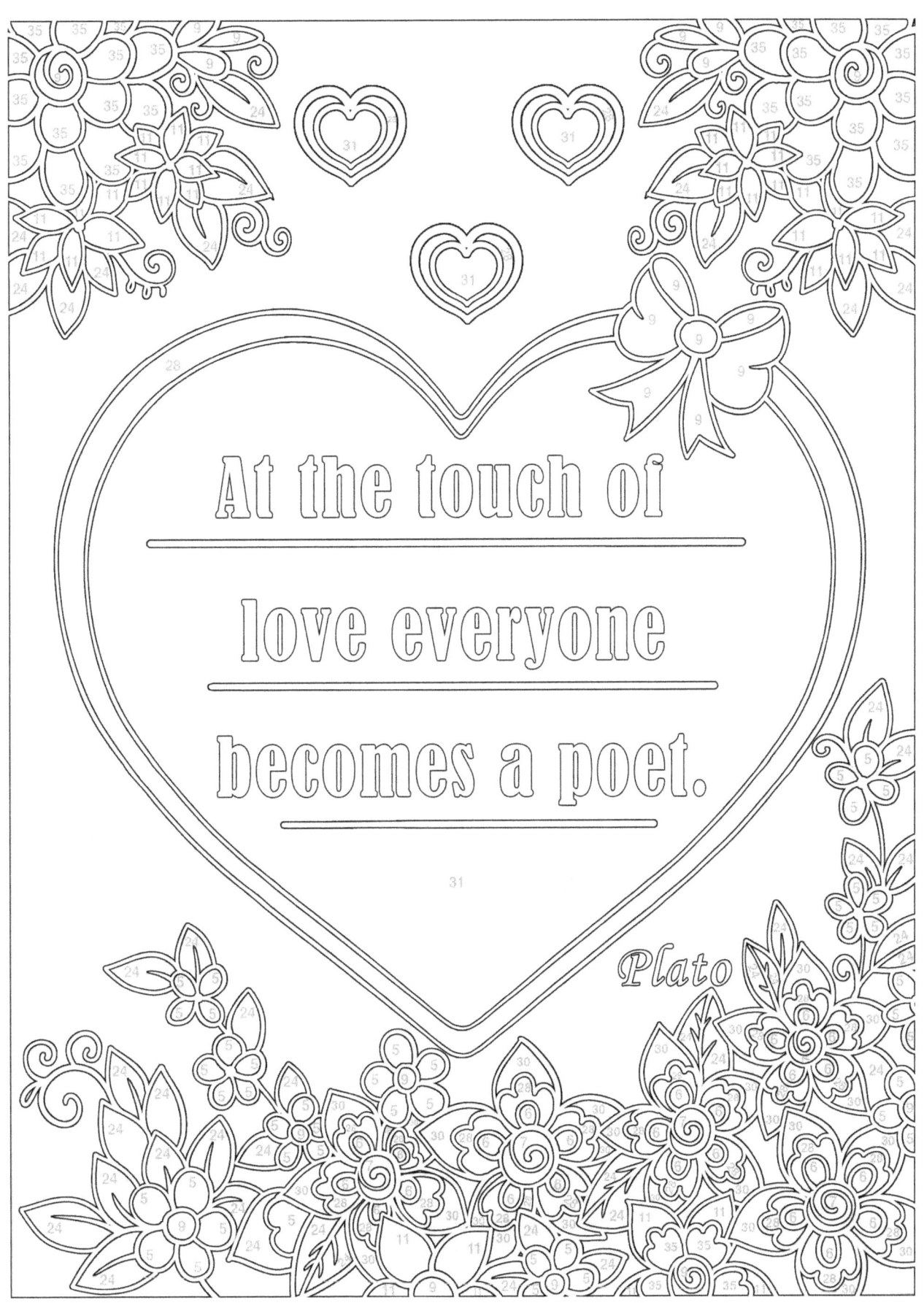

5. Red

9. Yellow

14. Orange

16. Chocolate

22. Light Green

24. Green

28. Light Pink

31. Hot Pink

32. Dark Pink

33. Medium Purple

37. Violet

42. Medium Blue

3. Light Red

5. Red

9. Yellow

11. Bright Orange

12. Light Orange

14. Orange

16. Chocolate

22. Light Green

24. Green

25. Army Green

28. Light Pink

30. Pink

34. Purple

37. Violet

42. Medium Blue

43. Blue

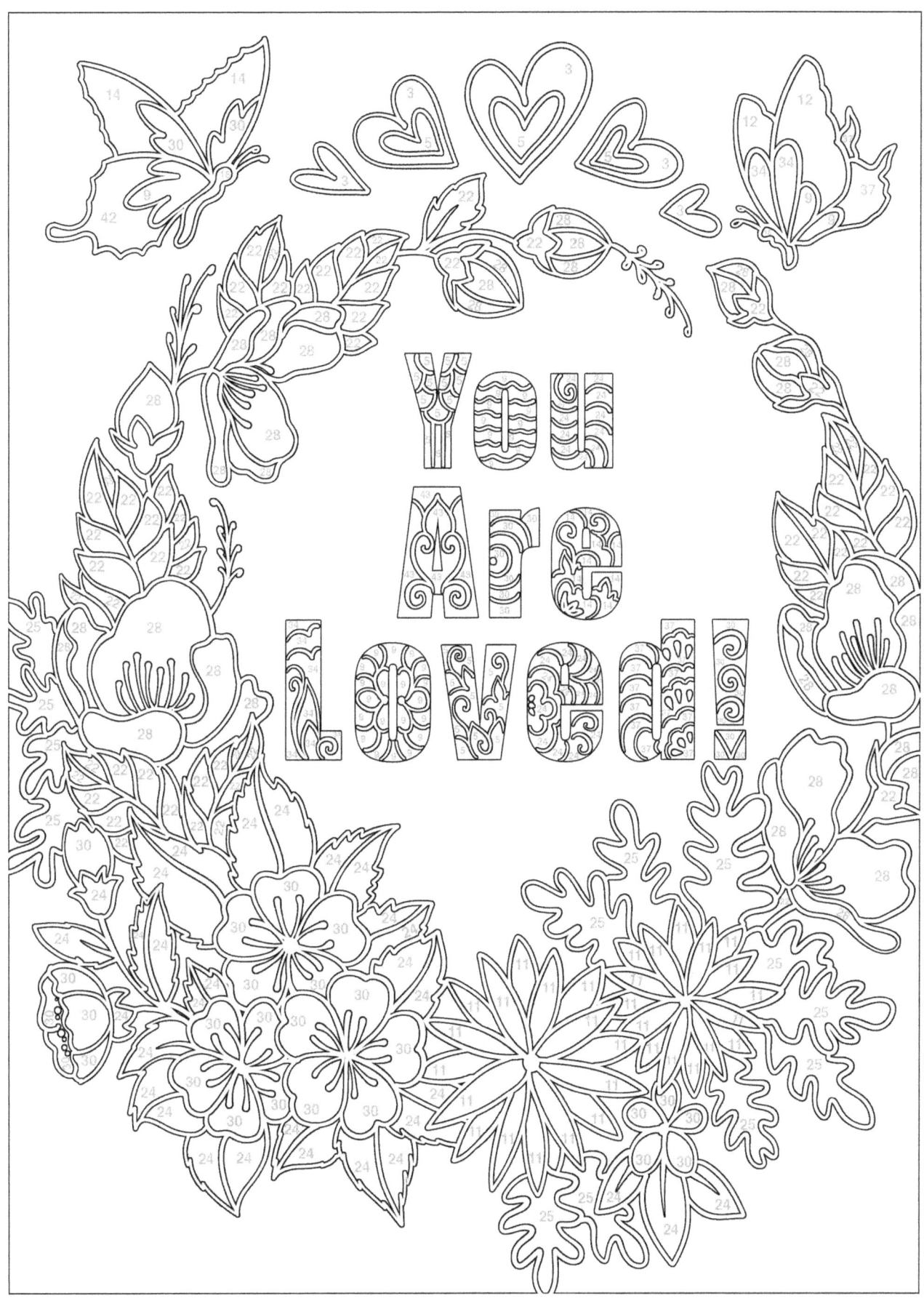

5. Red

9. Yellow

12. Light Orange

14. Orange

24. Green

28. Light Pink

30. Pink

34. Purple

36. Soft Violet

37. Violet

ENJOY BONUS IMAGES FROM SOME OF OUR OTHER FUN COLOR BY NUMBER BOOKS!

FIND ALL OF OUR BOOKS ON AMAZON

Beautiful Hummingbirds
Mosaic Color By Number
Coloring Book For Adults

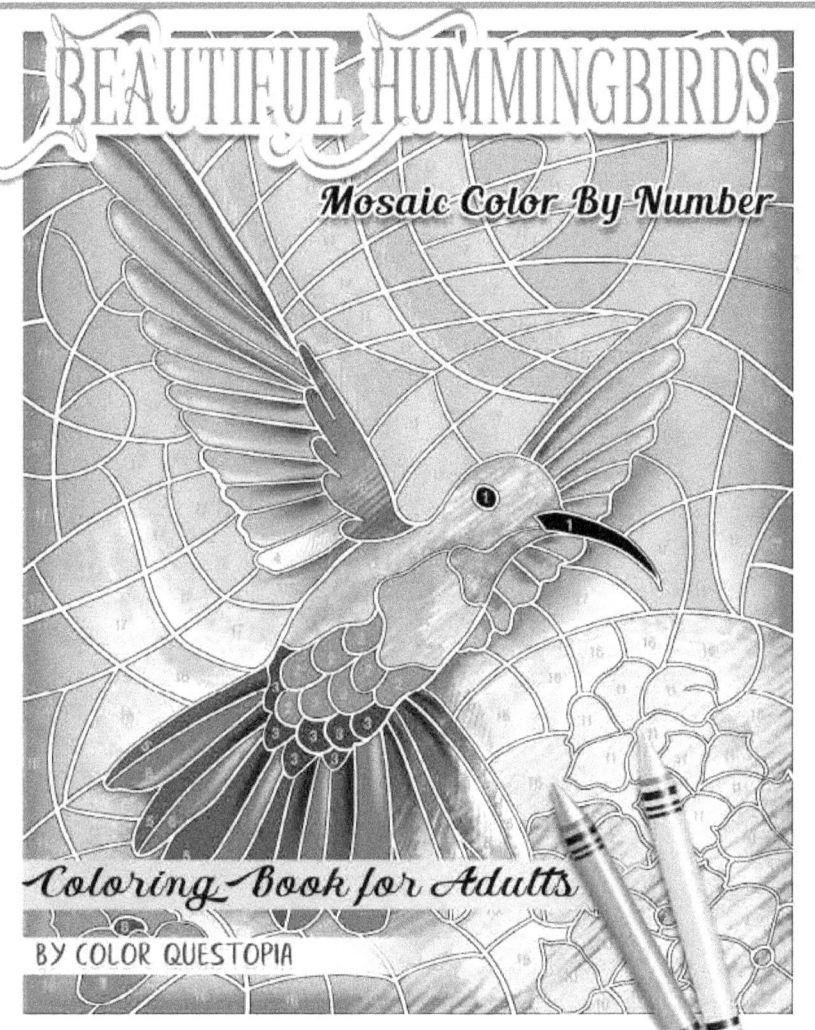

1. Black
2. Purple
3. Dark Brown
4. Yellow
5. Orange
6. Blue
7. Bright Orange
8. Green
9. Light Brown
10. Brown
11. Pink
12. Light Pink
13. Light Green
14. Red
15. Light Violet
16. Violet
17. Sky Blue

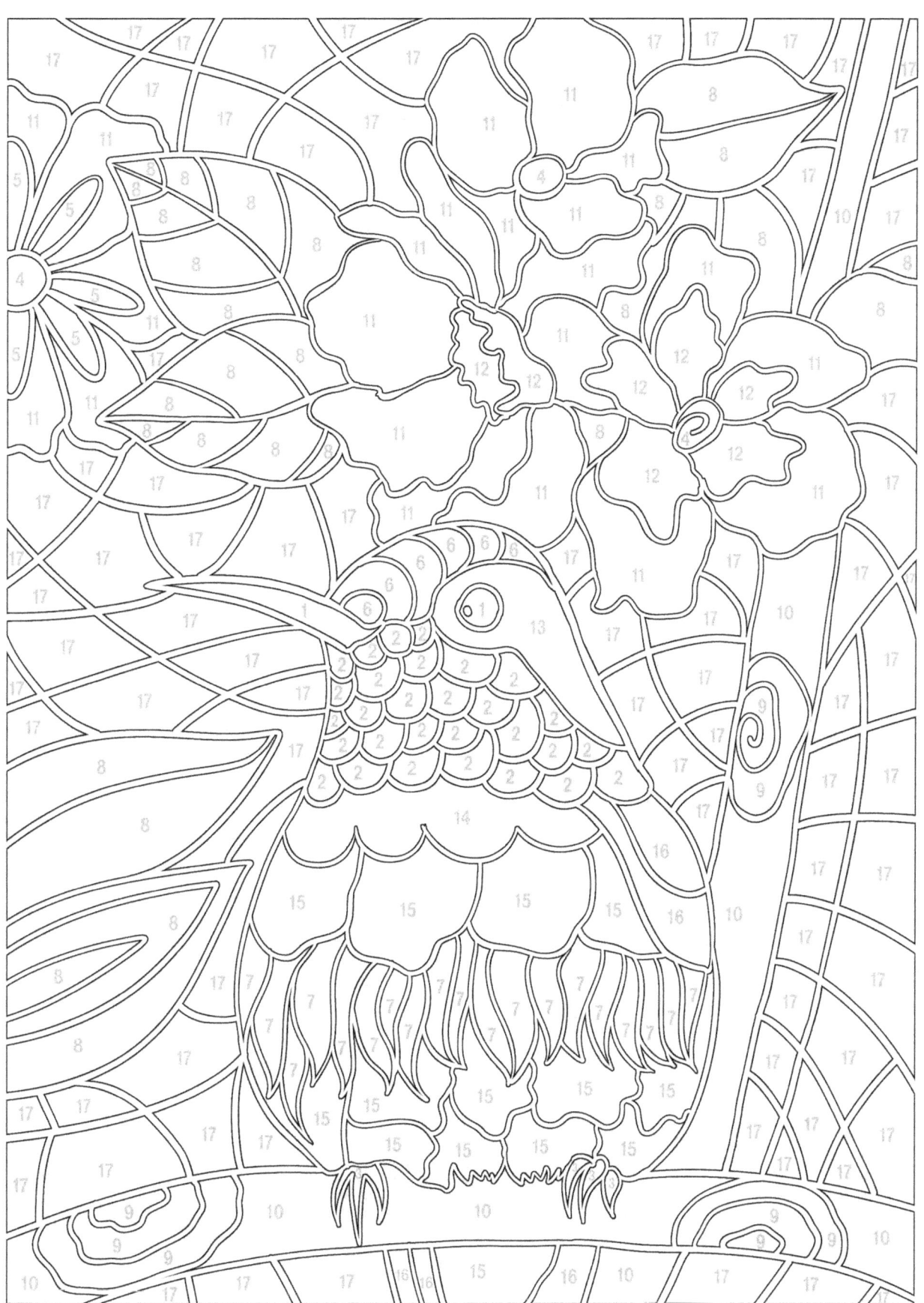

Princess Coloring Book
Large Print Mosaic
Color By Number

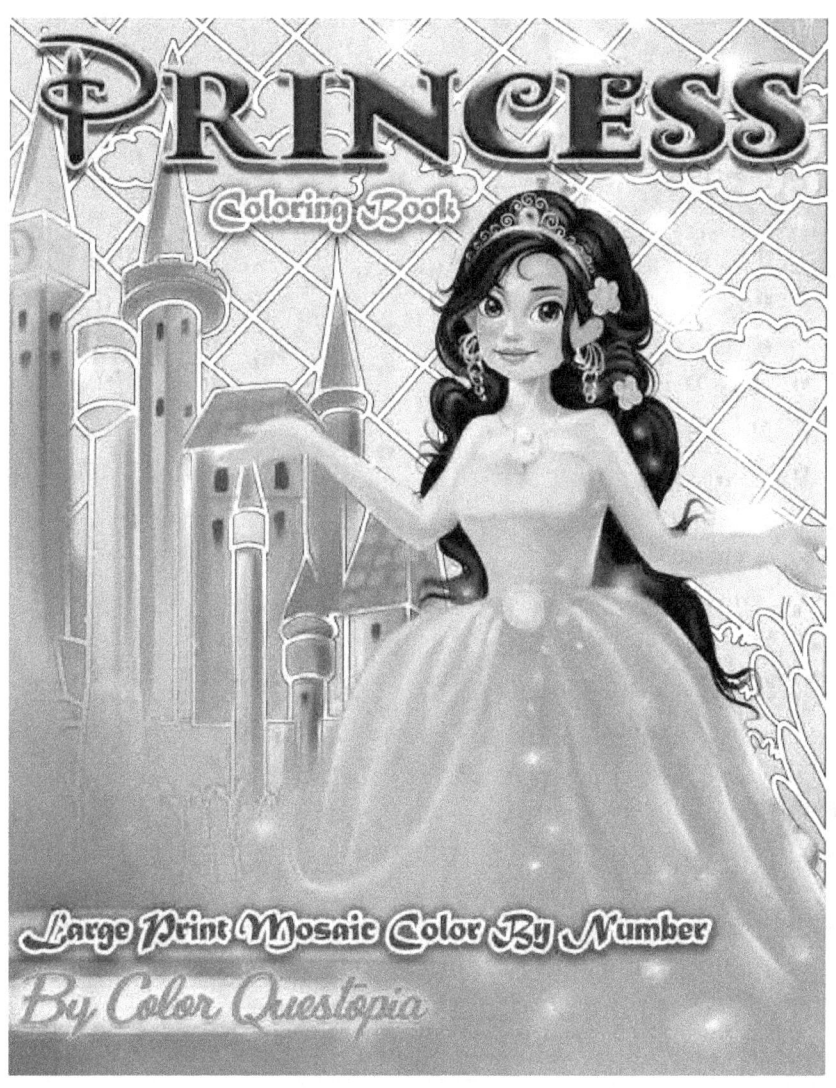

1. Black
2. Peach
3. Orange
4. Pink
5. Light Pink
6. Yellow
7. Red
8. Violet
9. Green
10. Beige
11. Soft Violet
12. Bright Orange
13. Light Yellow
14. Baby Blue
15. Sky Blue

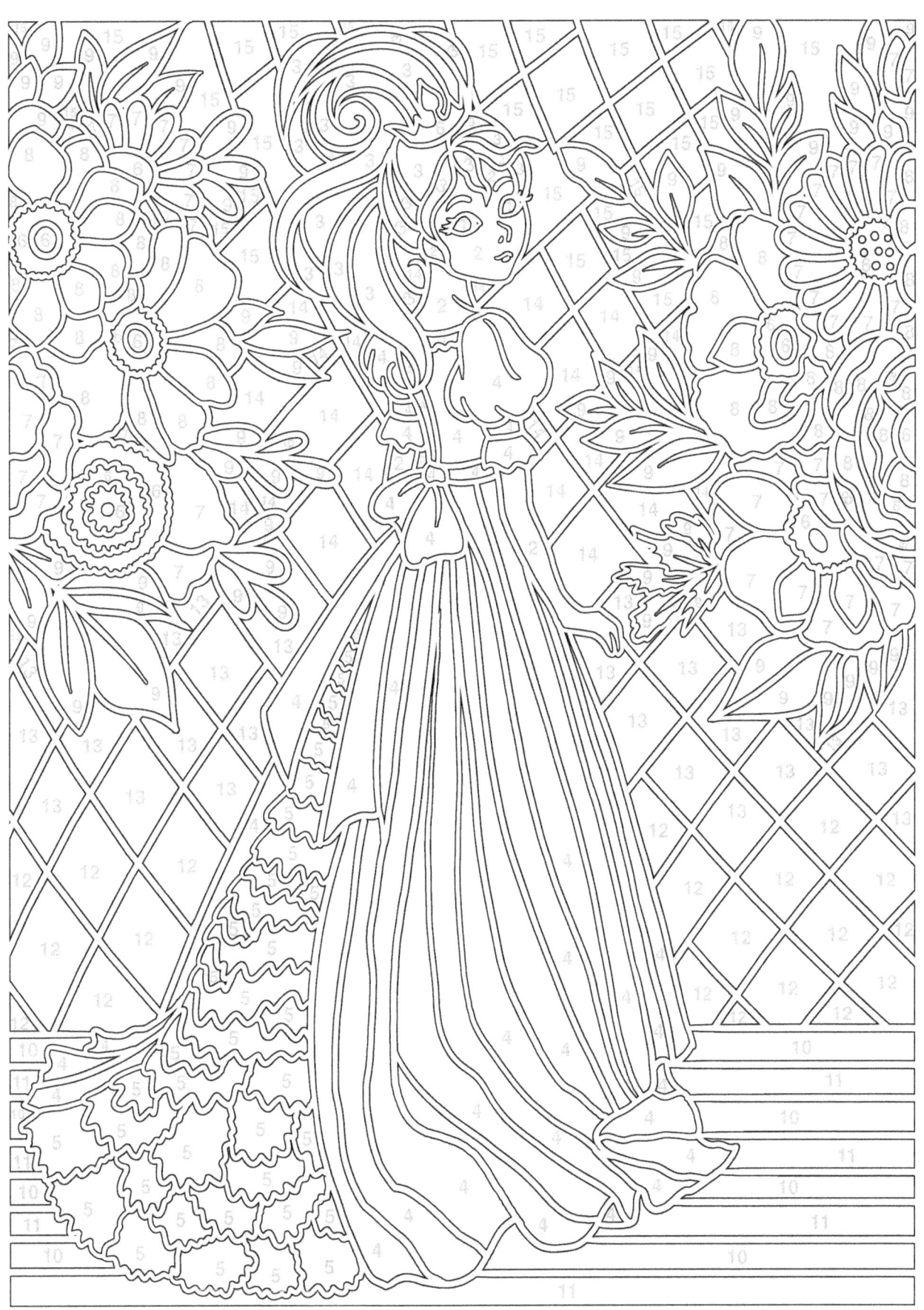

BEAUTIFUL PANDAS
Color By Number
A Mosaic Adult Coloring Book

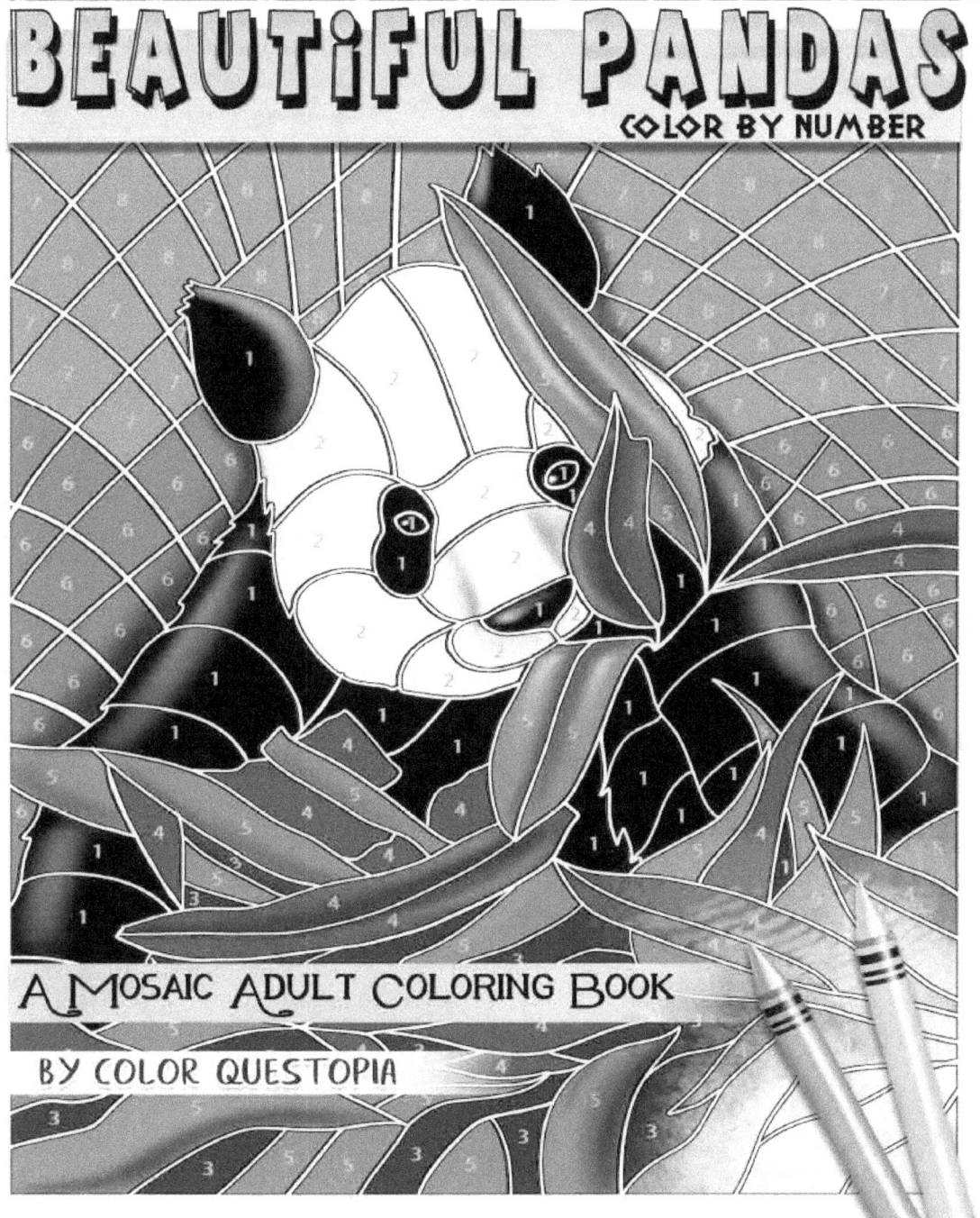

1. Black
2. Dark Brown
3. White
4. Light Gray
5. Brown
6. Light Brown
7. Medium Brown
8. Green
9. Dark Green
10. Medium Green
11. Light Green
12. Neon Green

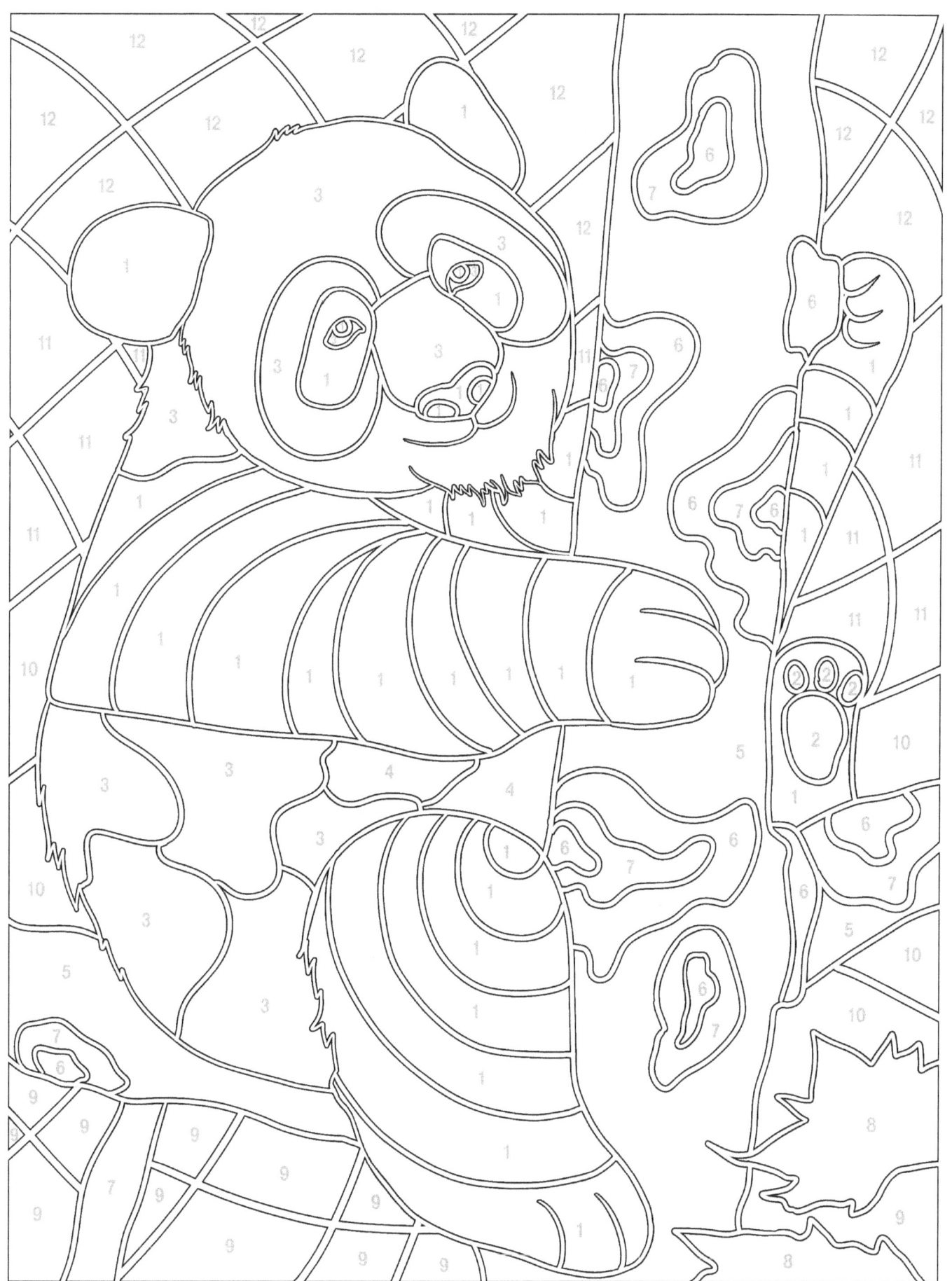

Significant Otter
An Adult Color By Number Coloring Book

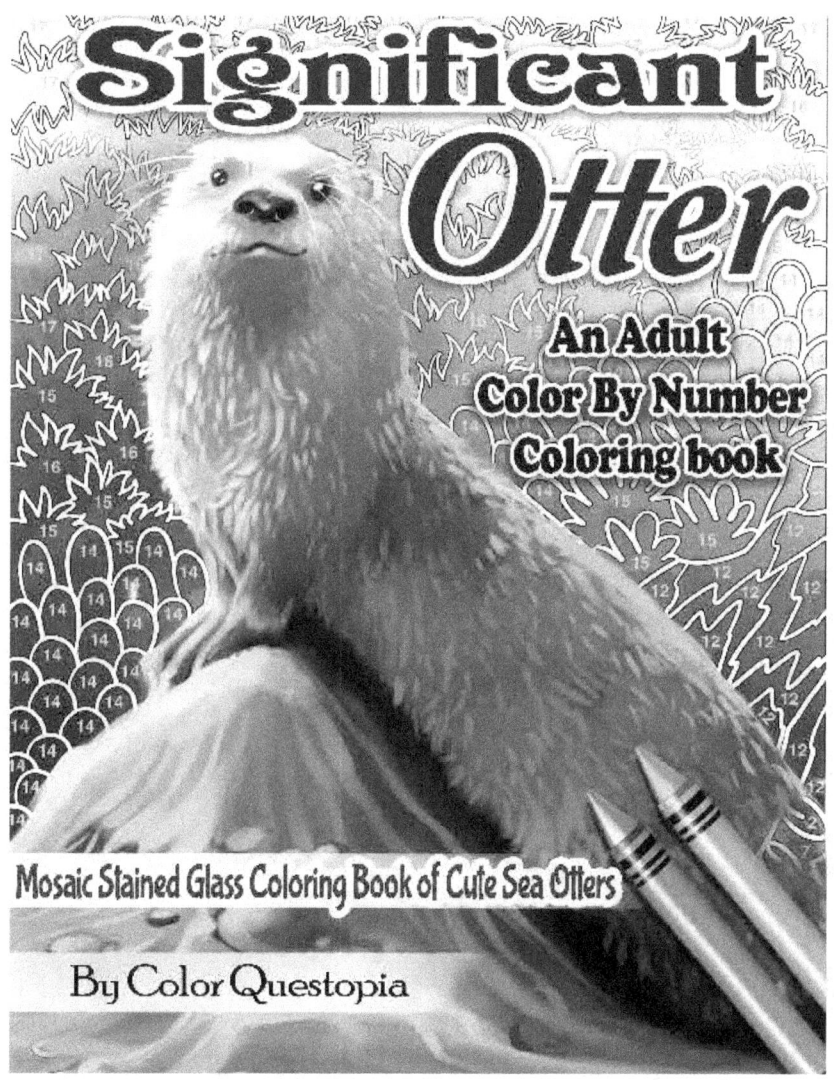

1. Pink
2. Orange
3. Violet
4. Blue
5. Red
6. Purple
7. Light Violet
8. Light Blue
9. Medium Purple
10. Black
11. Brown
12. Dark Blue
13. Green
14. Baby Blue
15. Soft Violet
16. Light Pink
17. Yellow

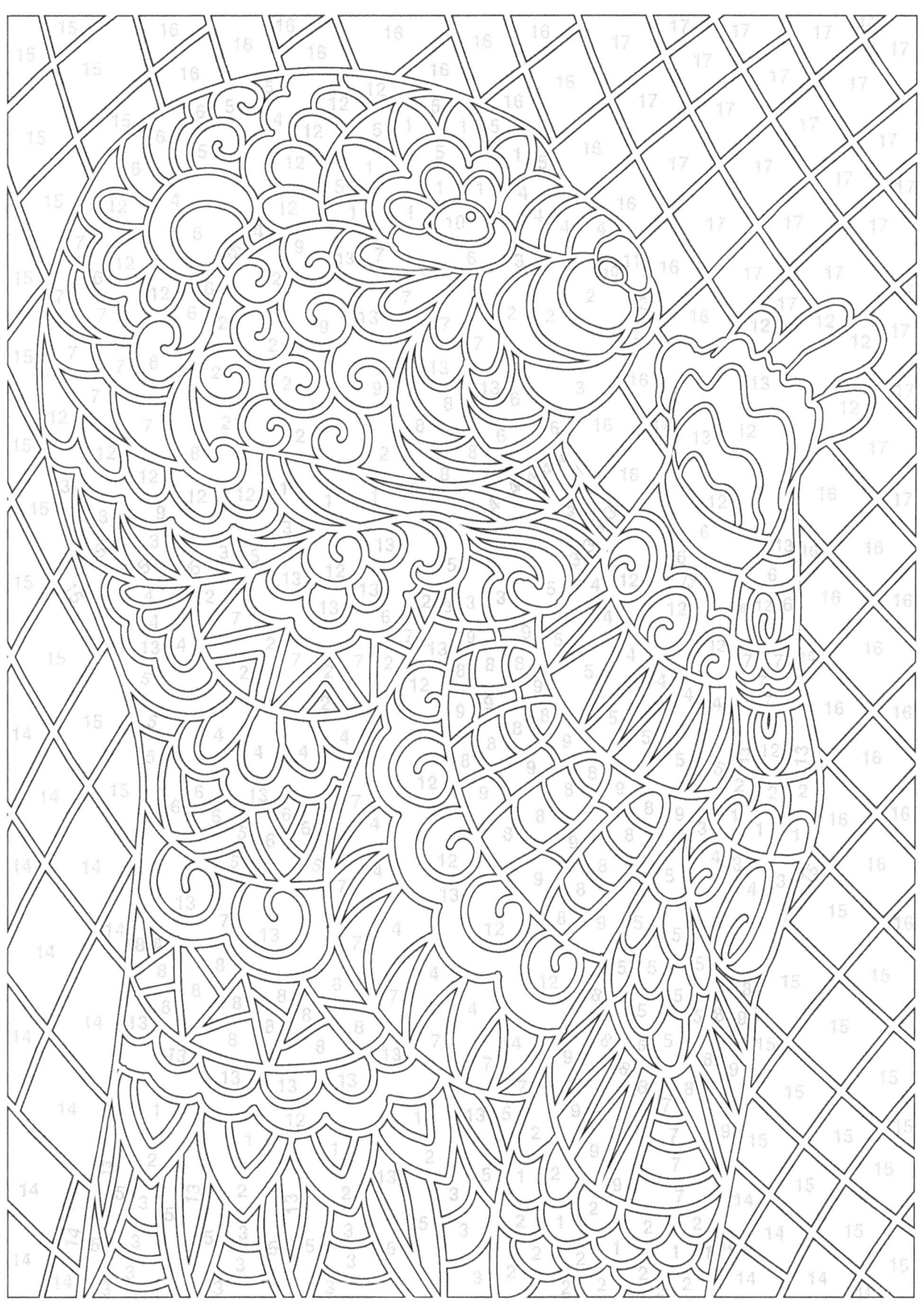

Fantasy Landscapes
Mosaic Color By Number Coloring Book for Adults

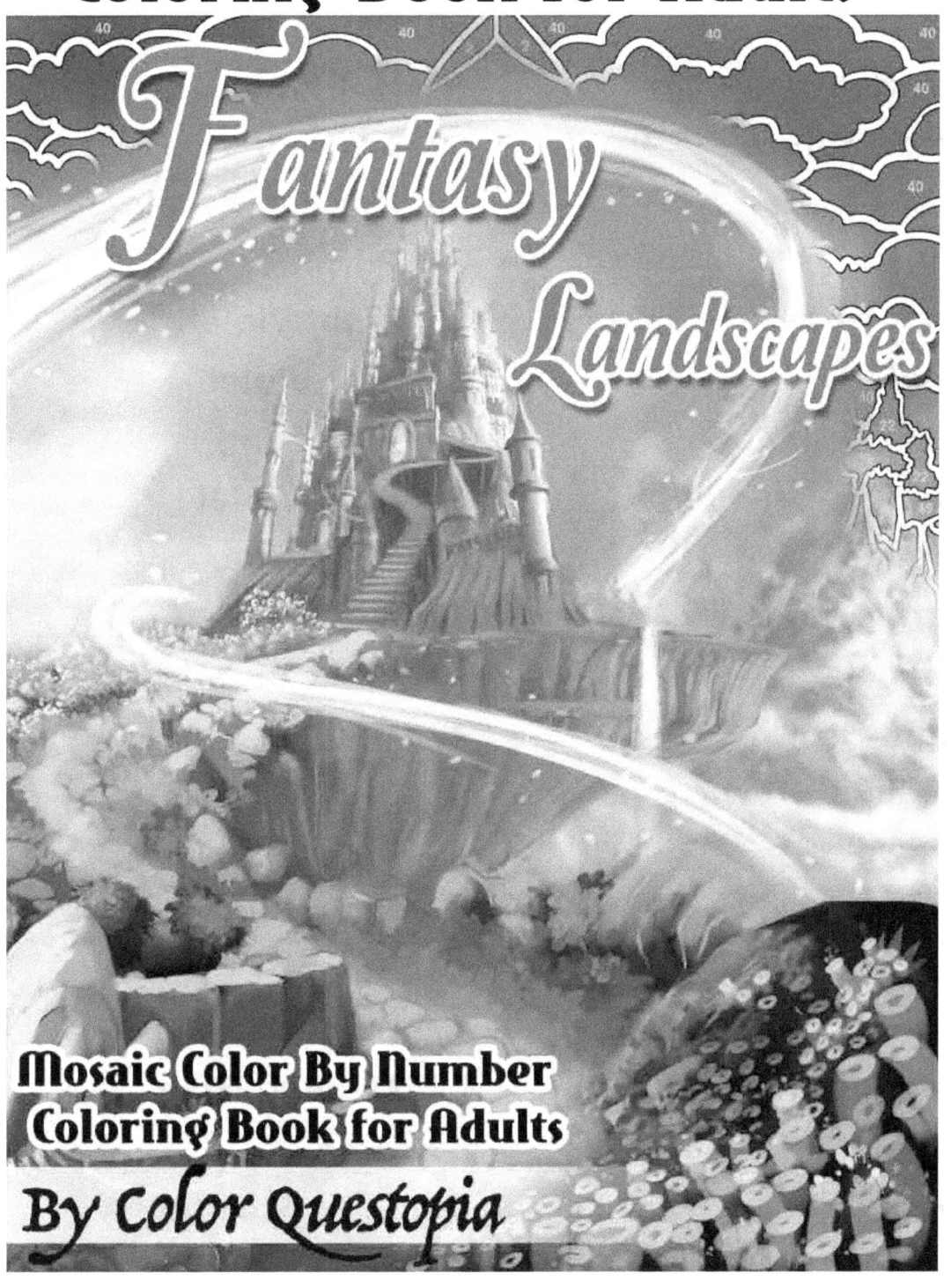

1. Black
2. Golden
3. Light Red
4. Medium Red
5. Red
6. Dark Red
7. Lemon Yellow
8. Light Yellow
9. Yellow
10. Dark Yellow
11. Bright Orange
12. Light Orange
13. Medium Orange
14. Orange
15. Dark Orange
16. Chocolate
17. Light Brown
18. Medium Brown
19. Brown
20. Dark Brown
21. Neon Green
22. Light Green
23. Medium Green
24. Green
25. Army Green
26. Dark Green
27. Peach
28. Light Pink
29. Medium Pink
30. Pink
31. Hot Pink
32. Dark Pink
33. Medium Purple
34. Purple
35. Light Violet
36. Soft Violet
37. Violet
38. Dark Violet
39. Baby Blue
40. Sky Blue
41. Light Blue
42. Medium Blue
43. Blue
44. Dark Blue
45. Navy Blue
46. Beige
47. Light Gray
48. Medium Gray
49. Gray
50. Dark Gray

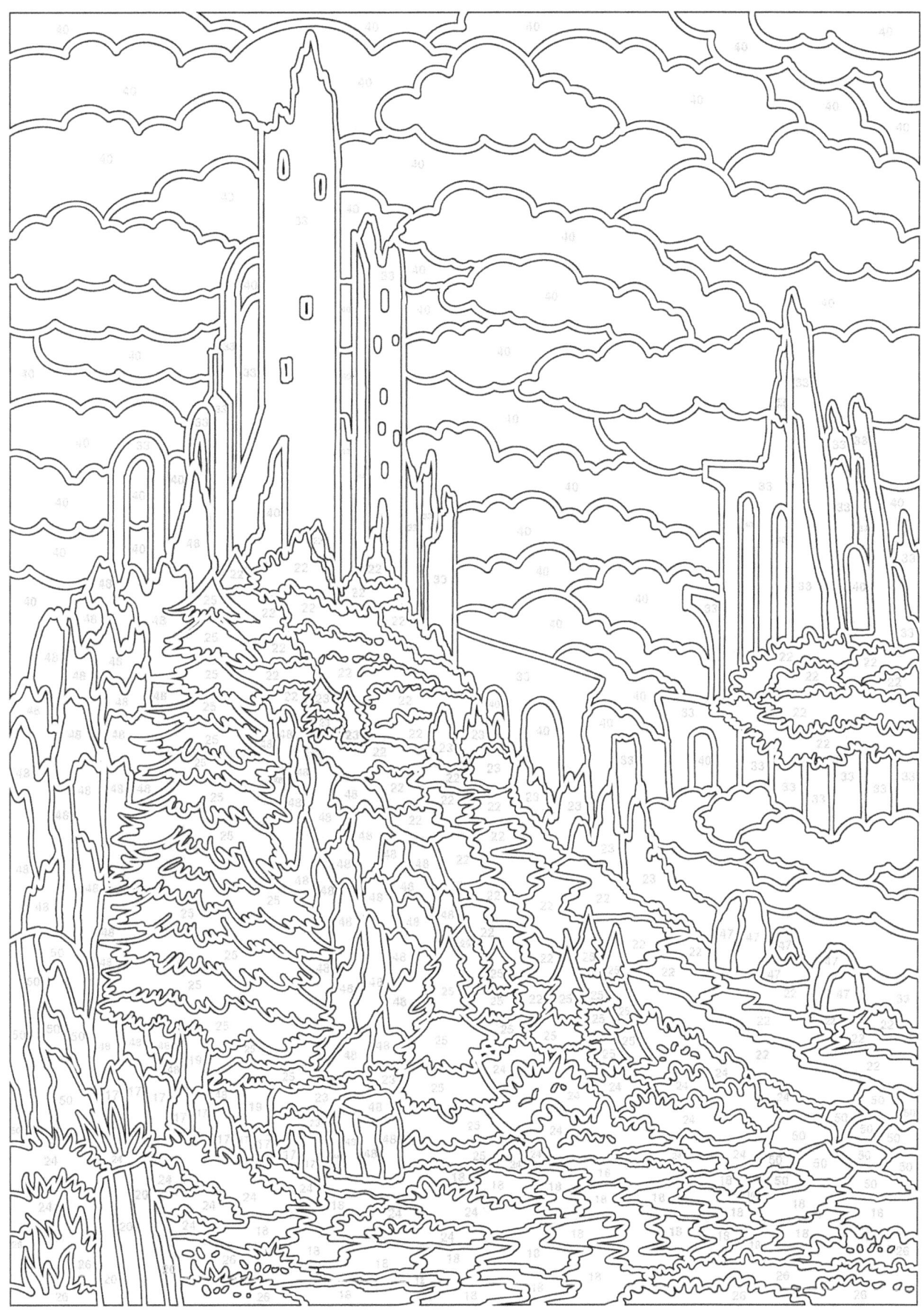

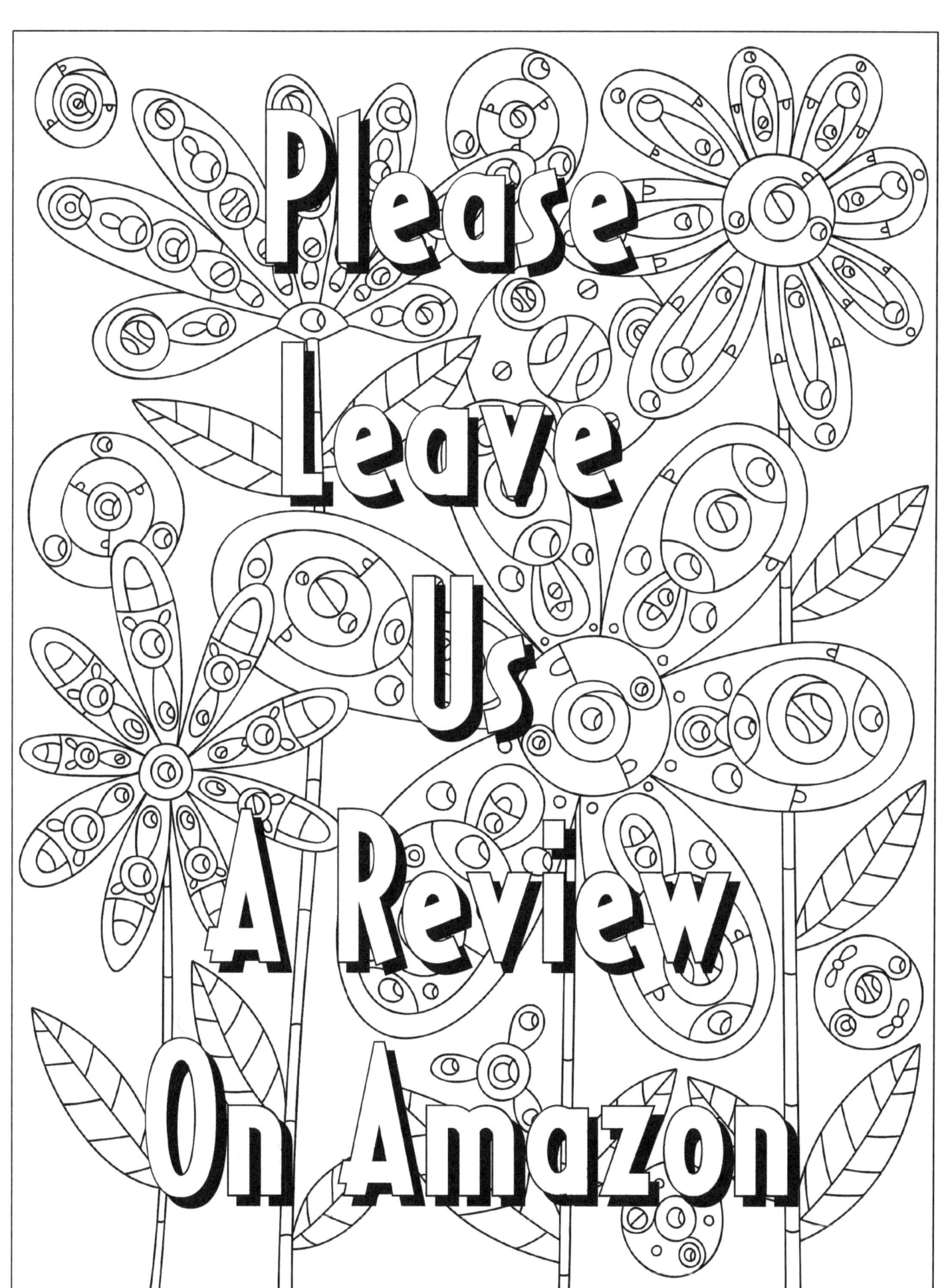

www.ingramcontent.com/pod-product-compliance
Lightning Source LLC
Chambersburg PA
CBHW081458220526
45466CB00008B/2696